this book

belongs to

A

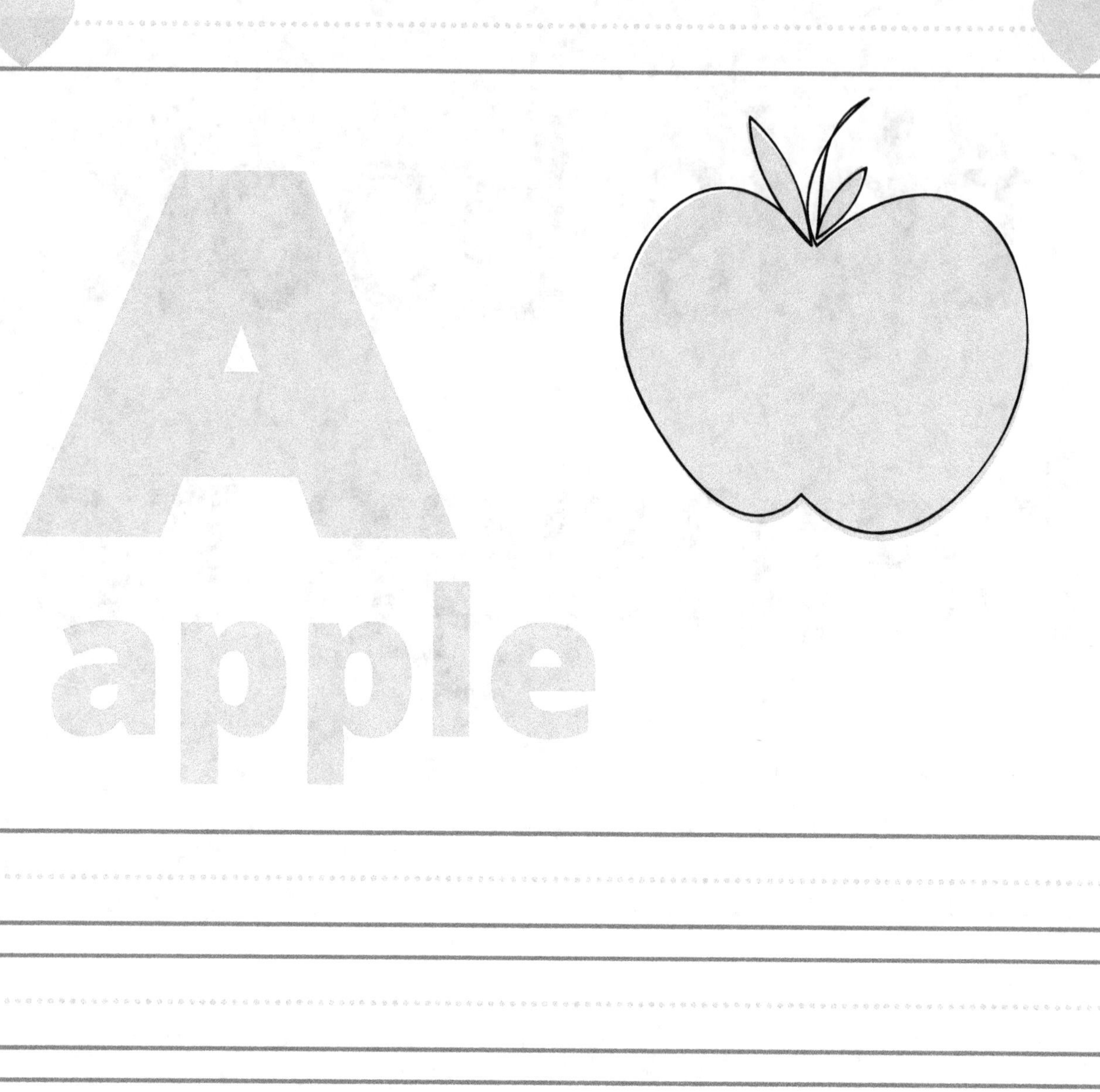

apple

B

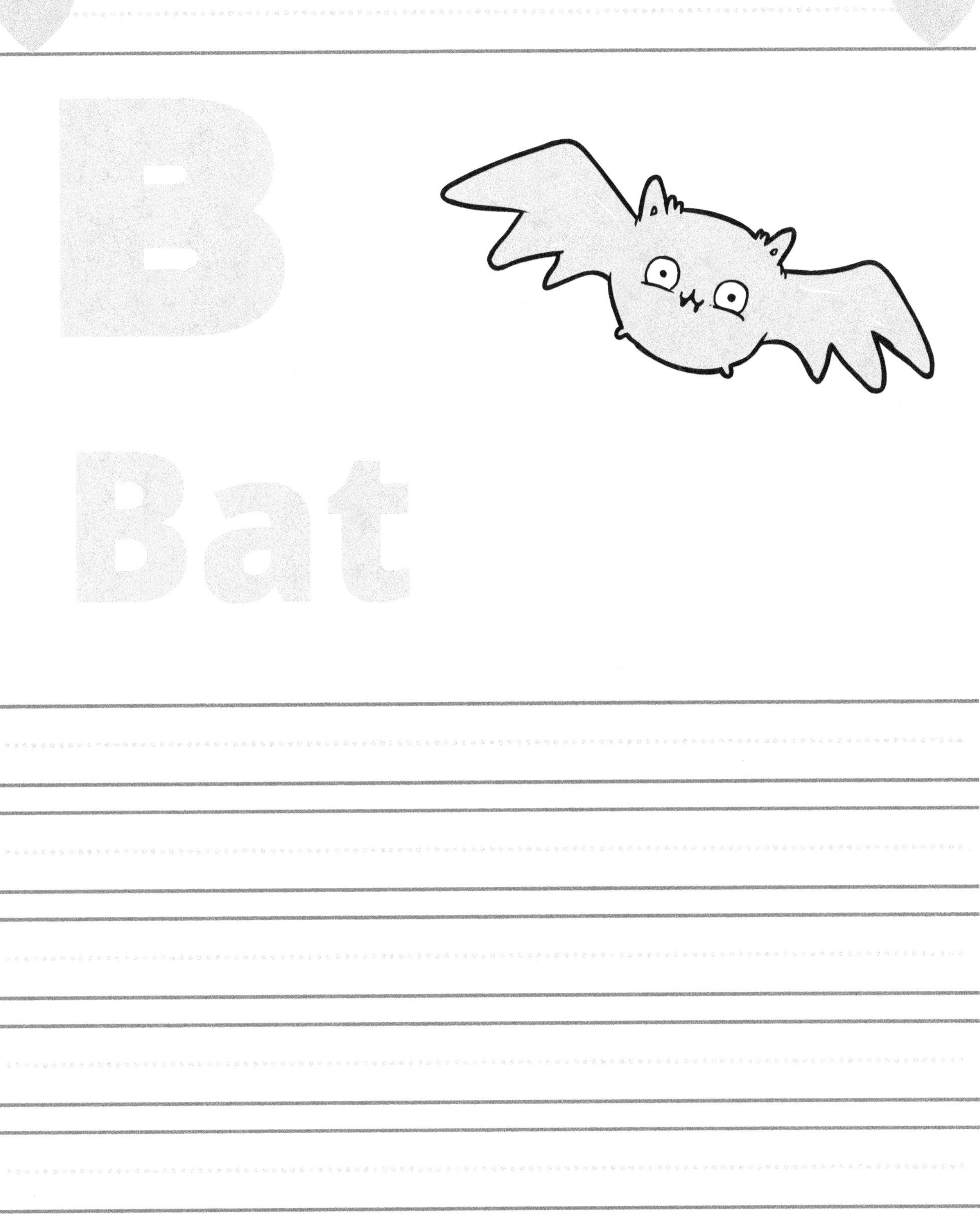

Bat

C

Cow

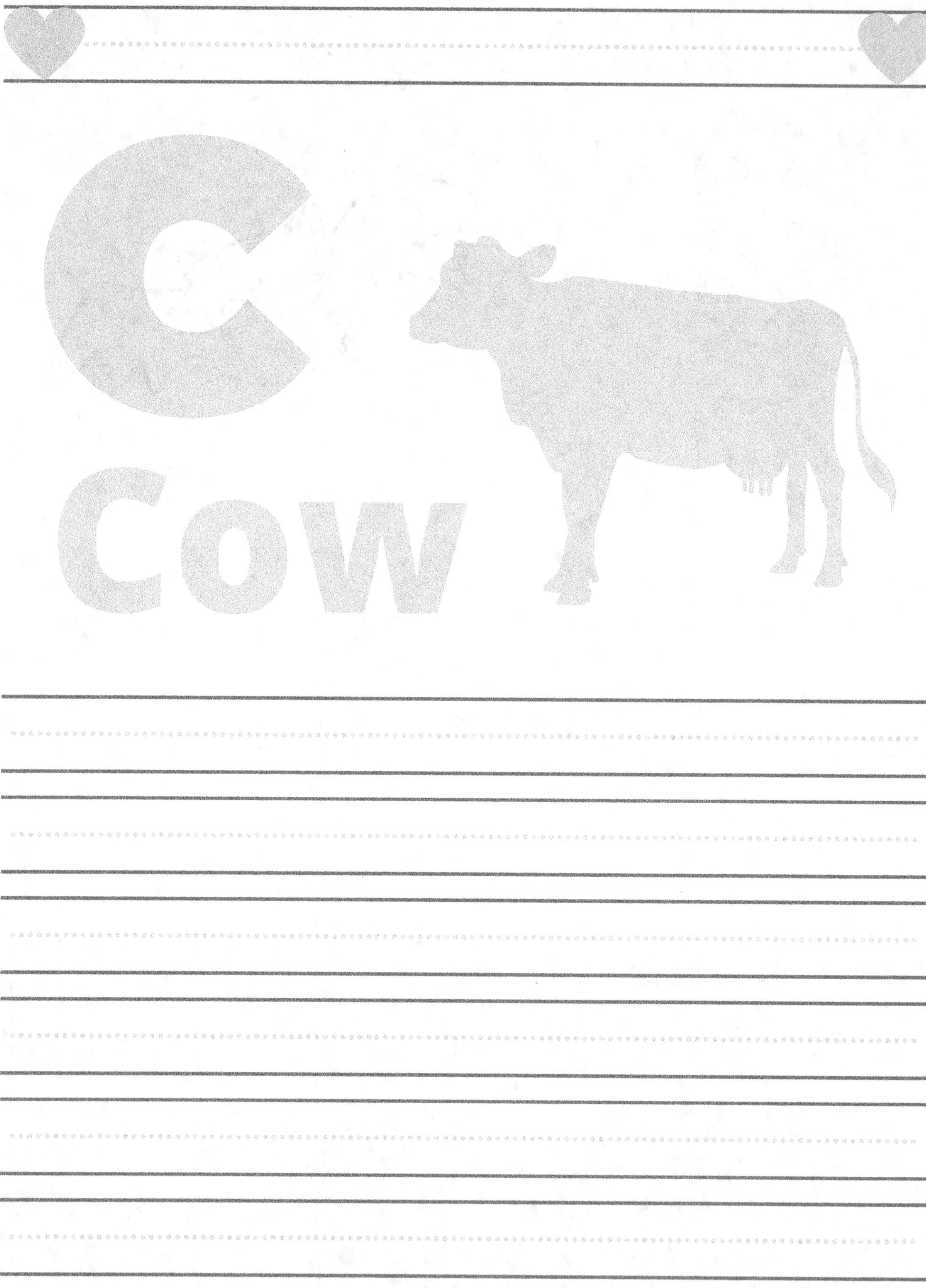

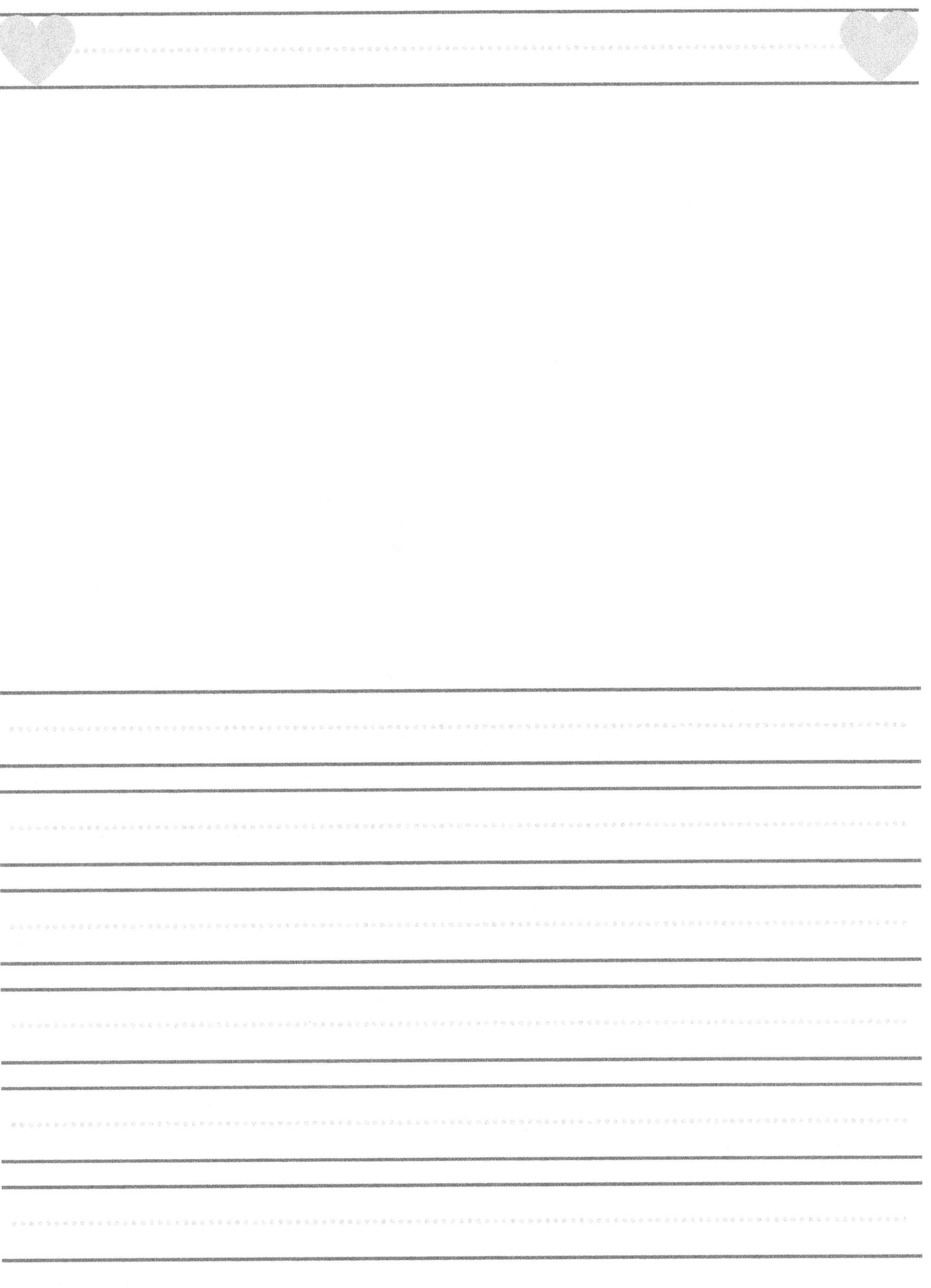

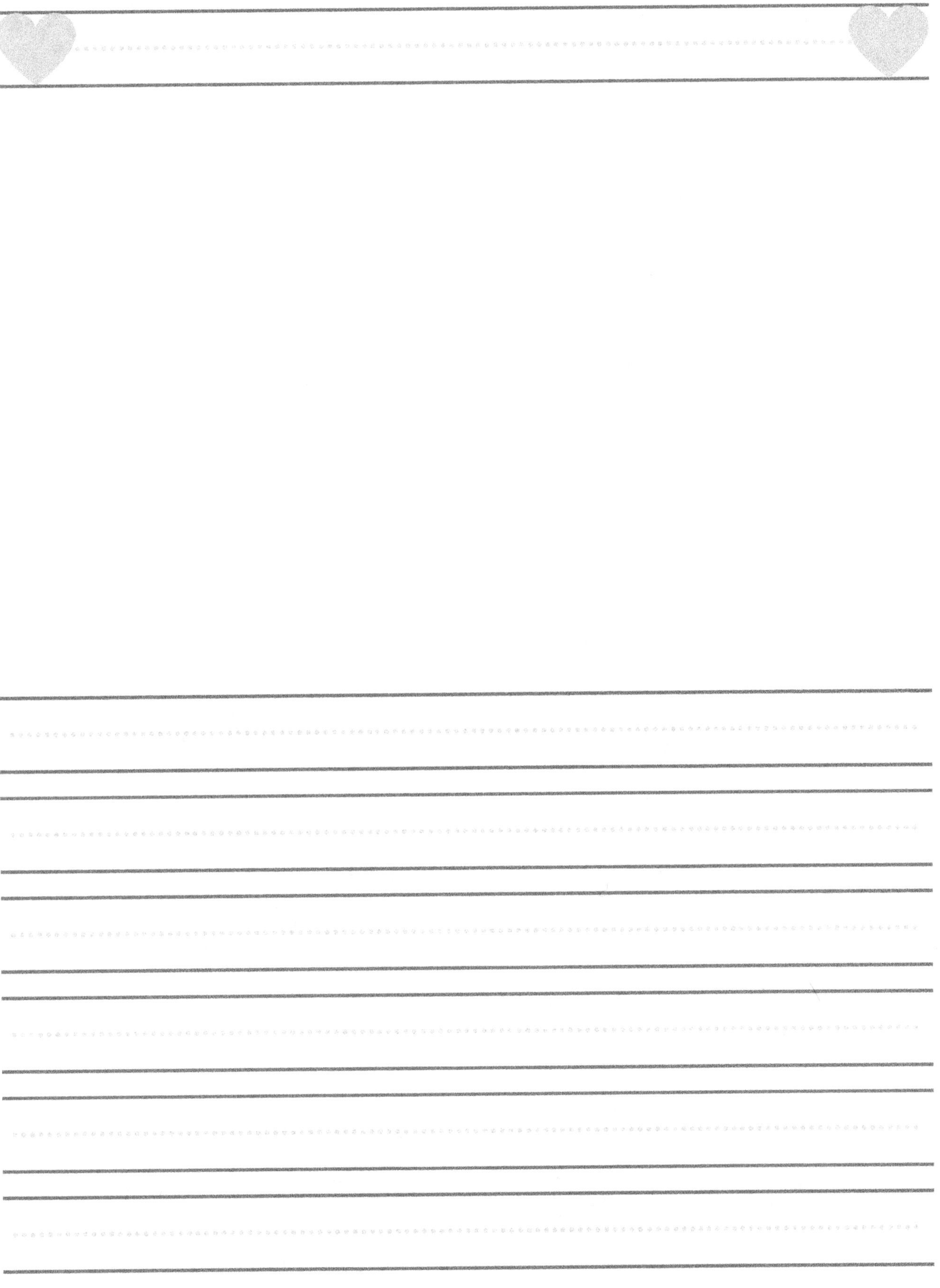

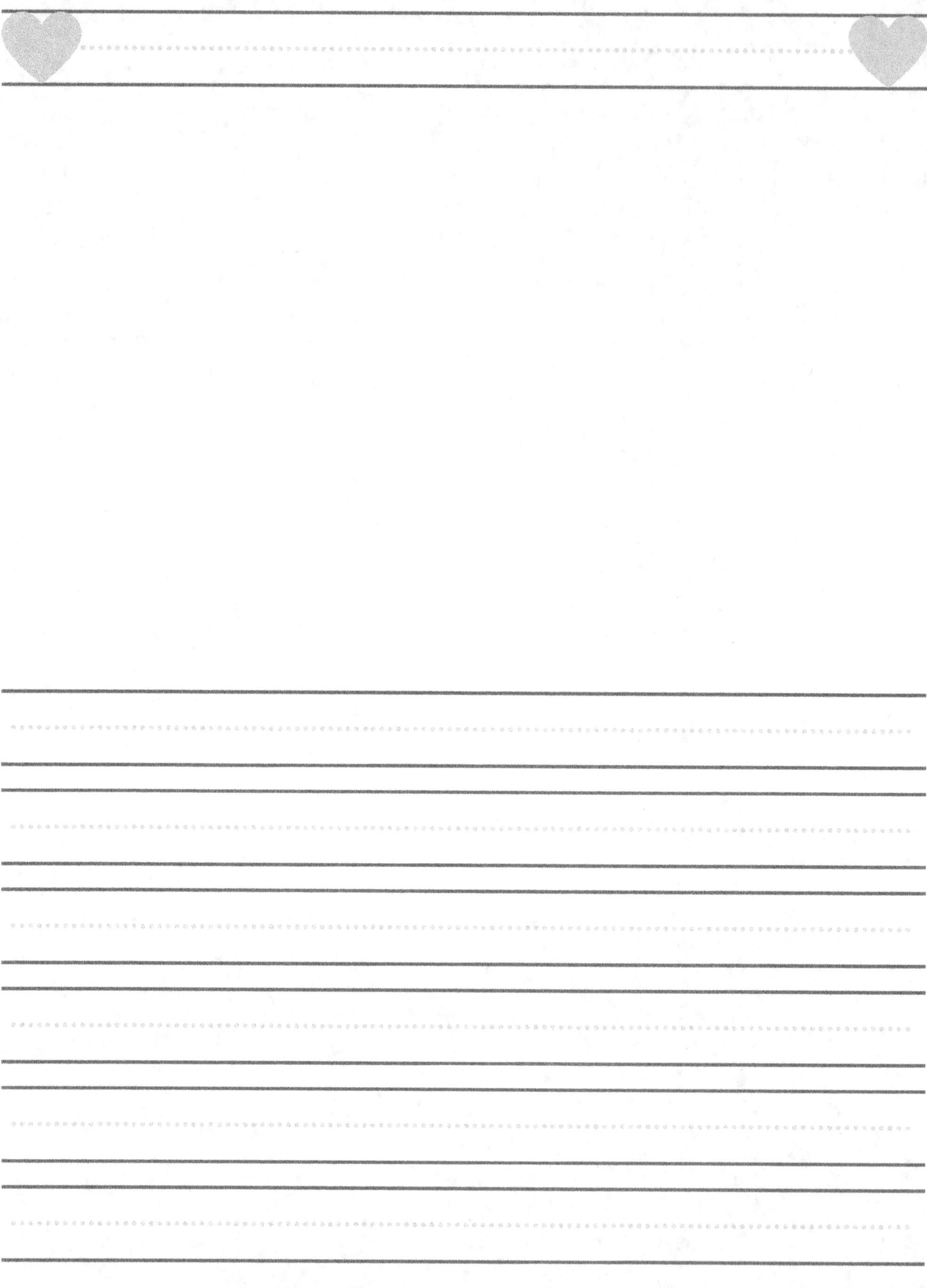

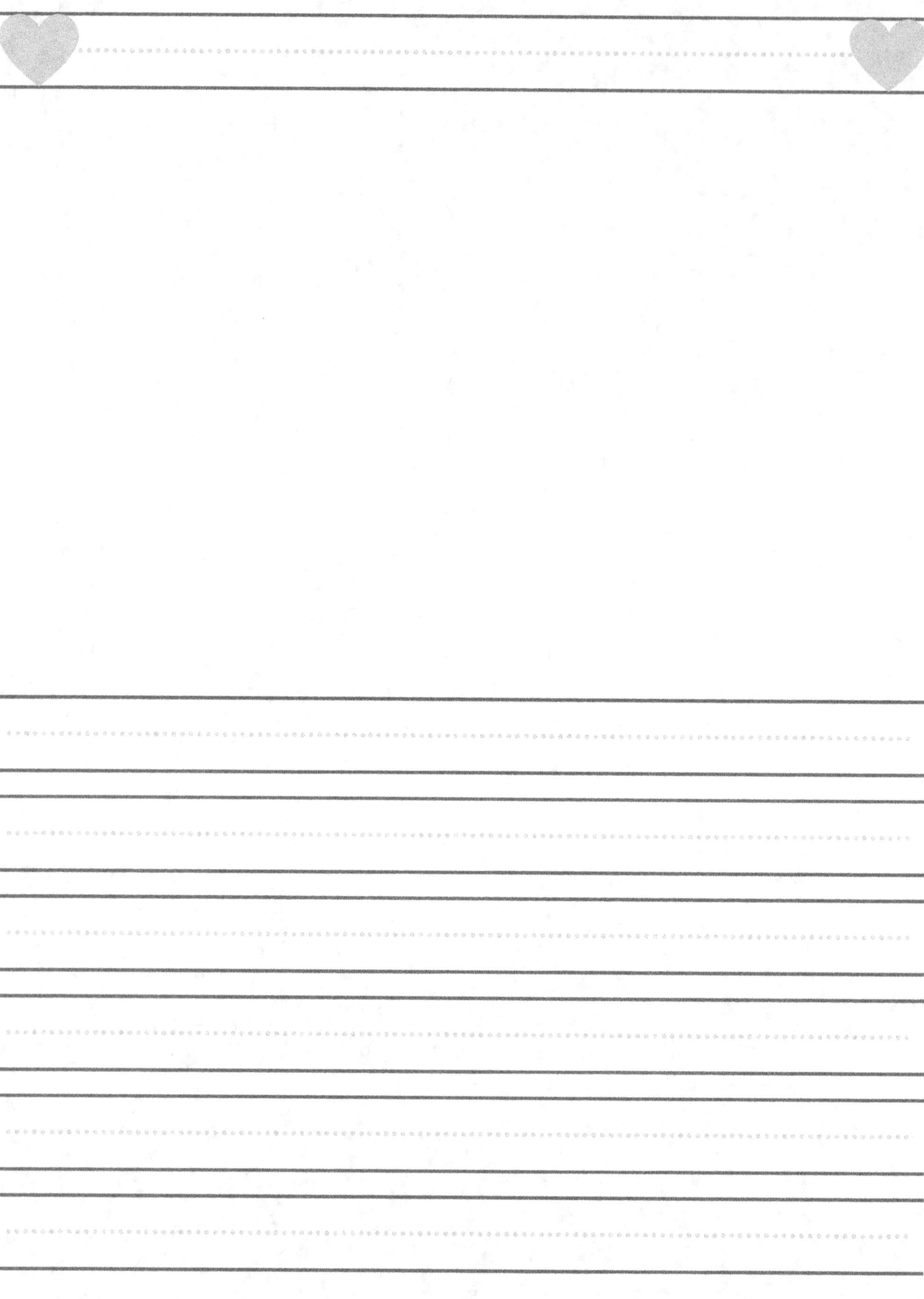

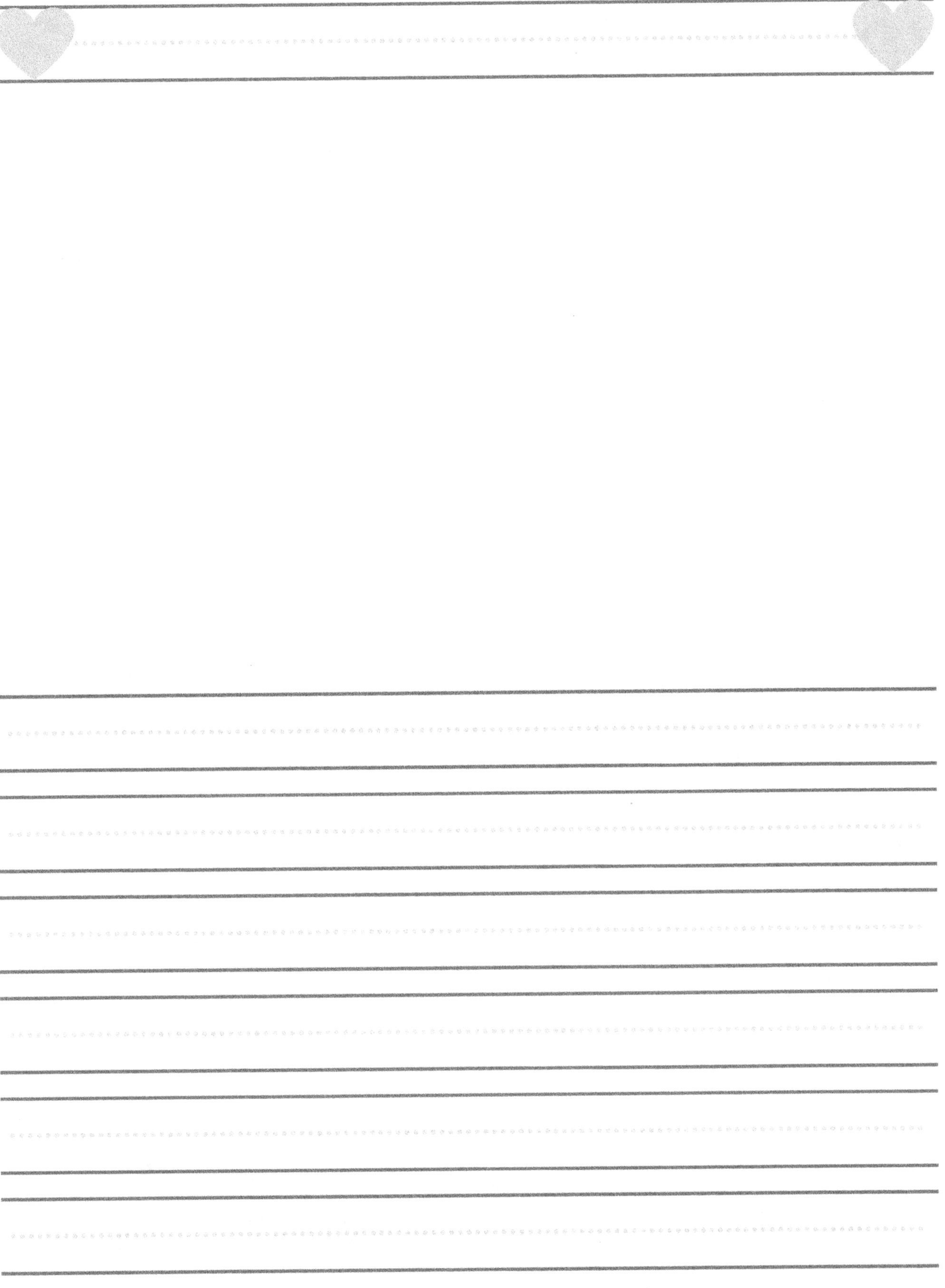

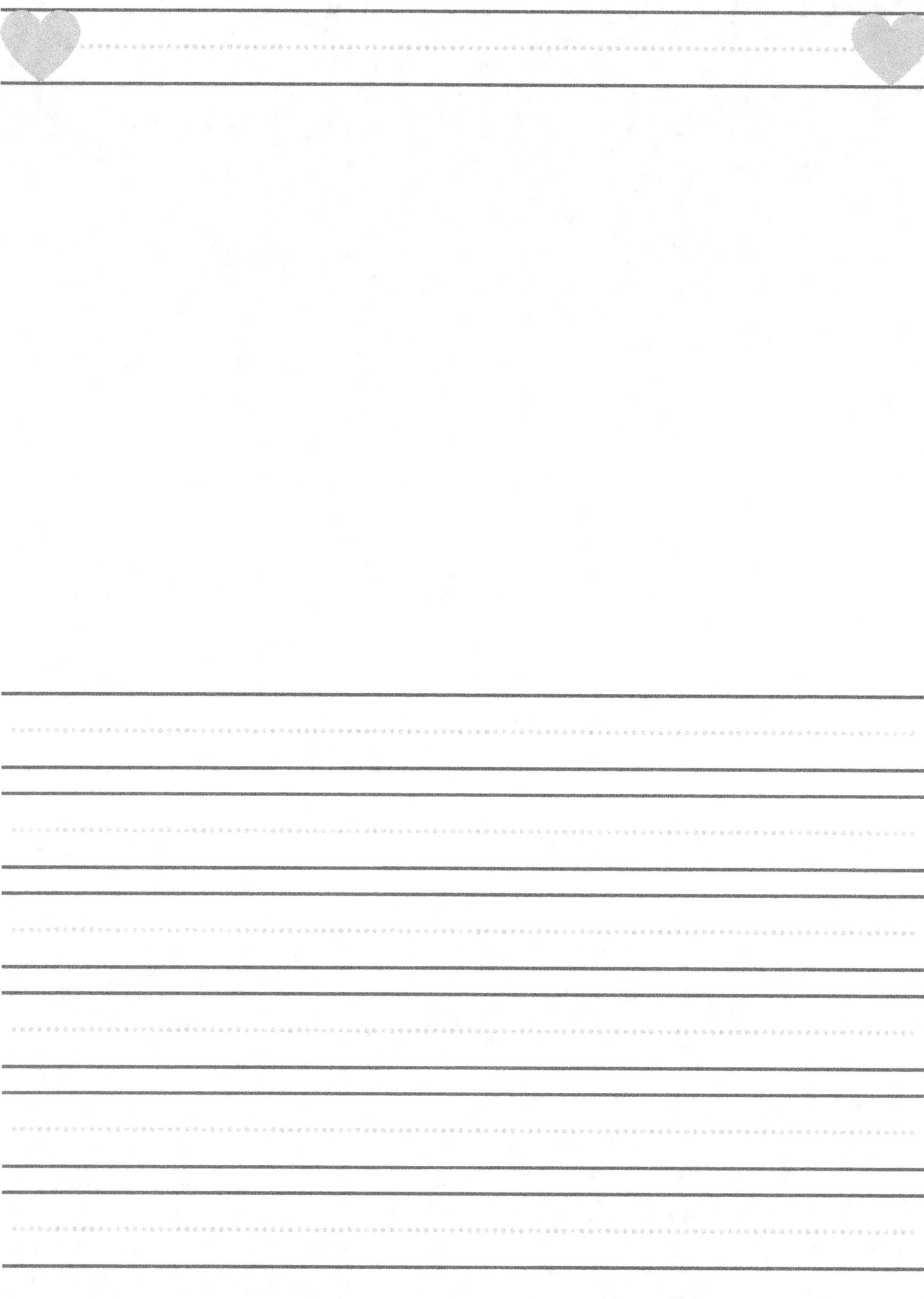

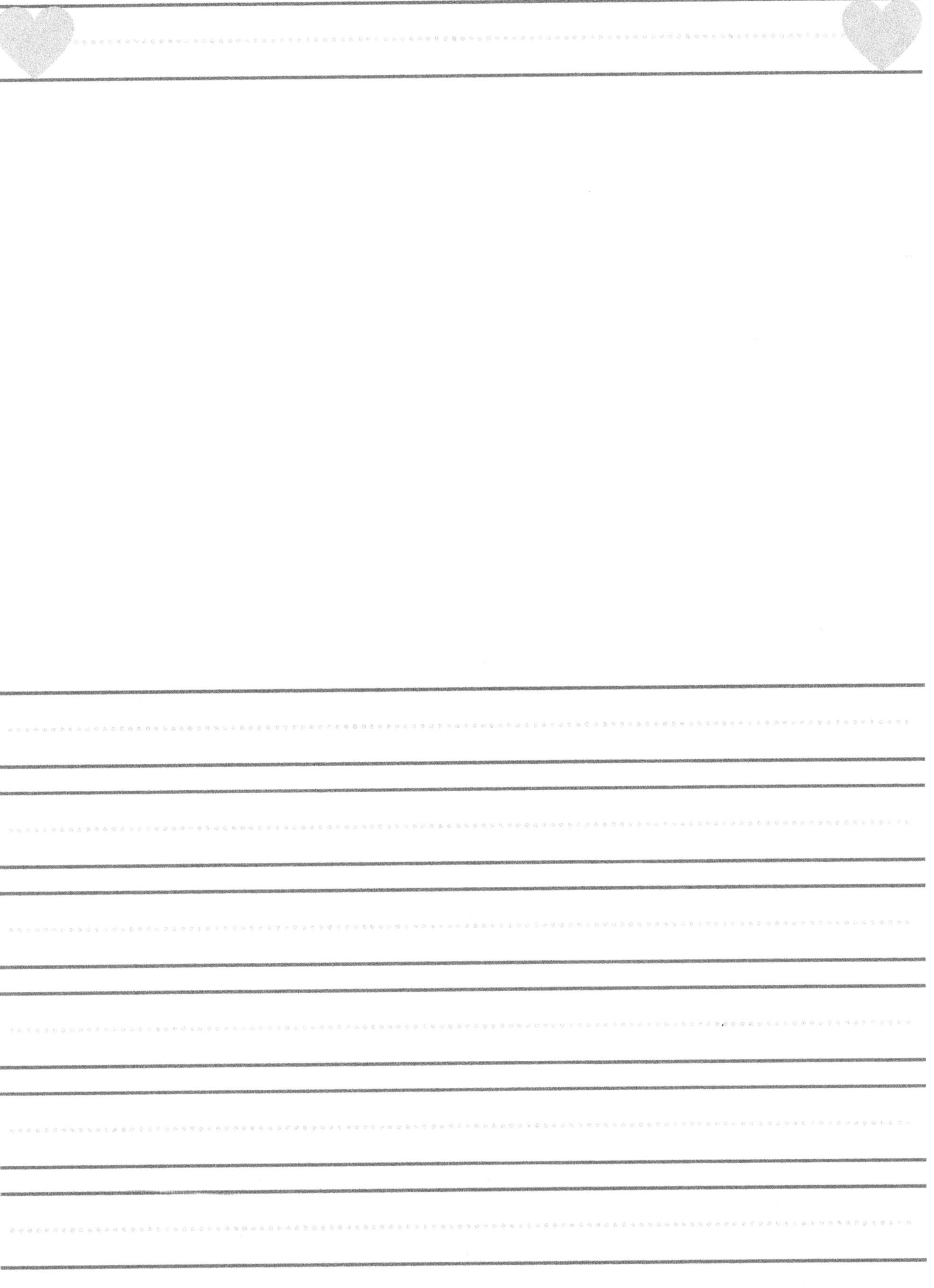

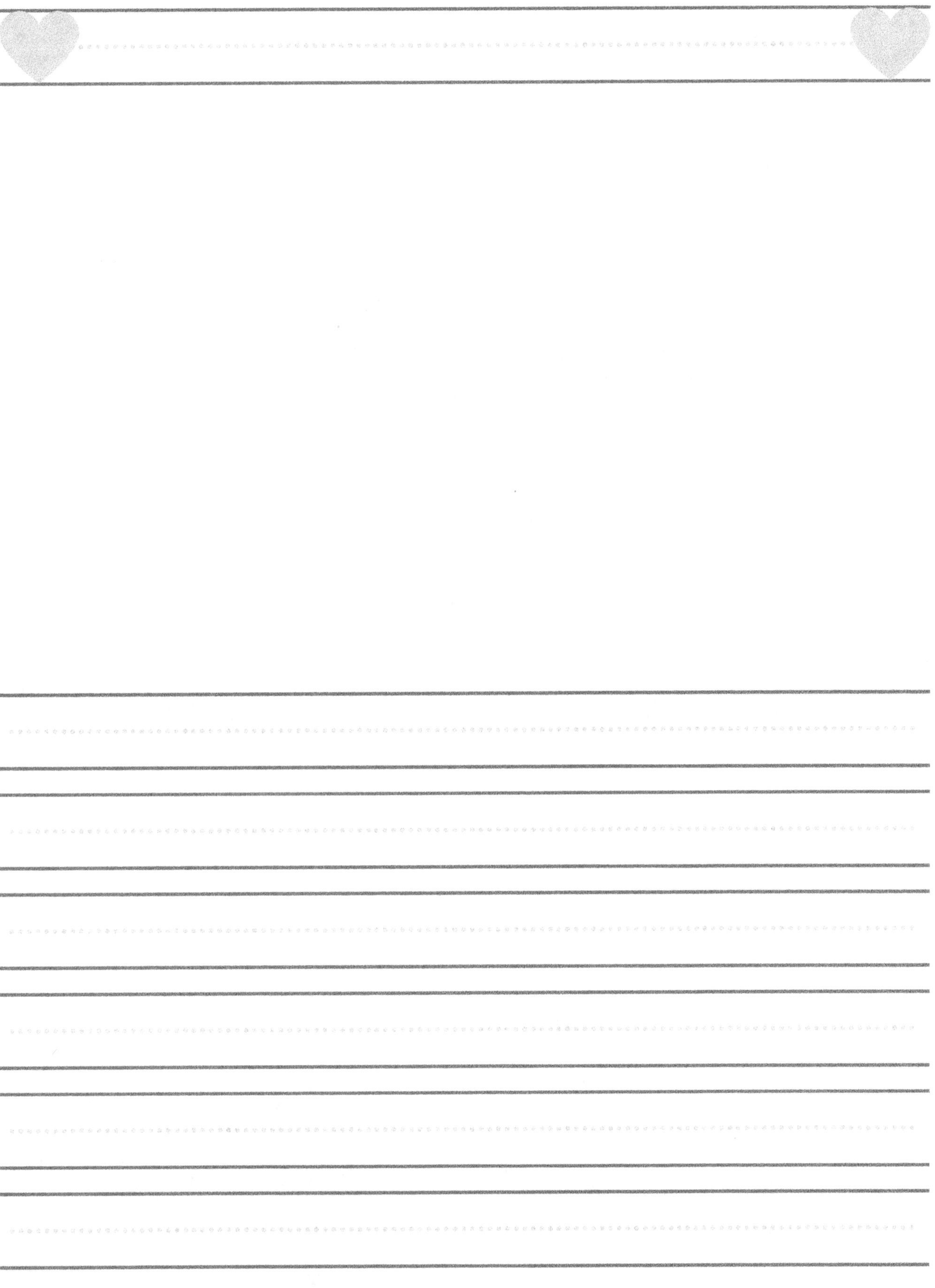

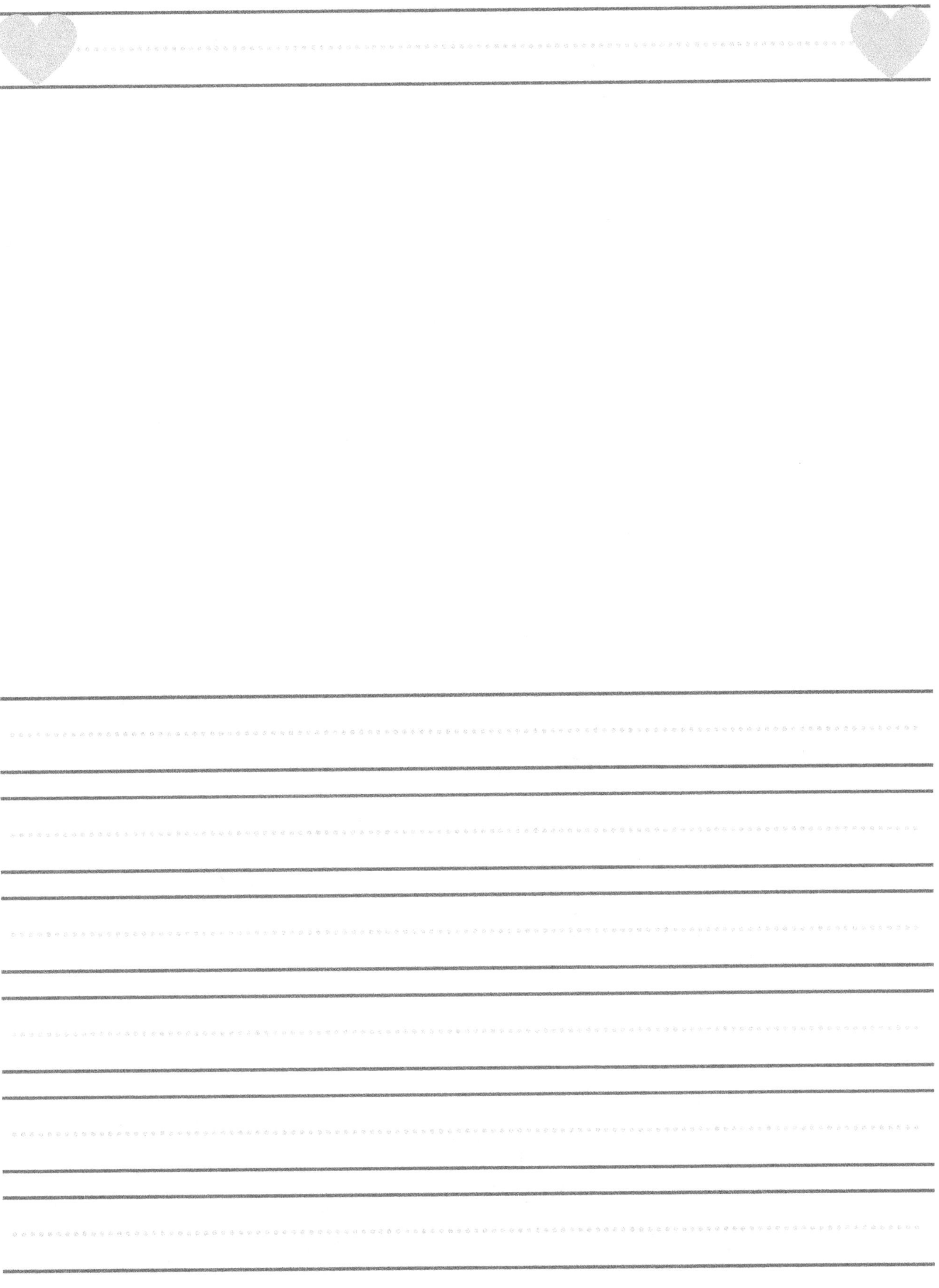

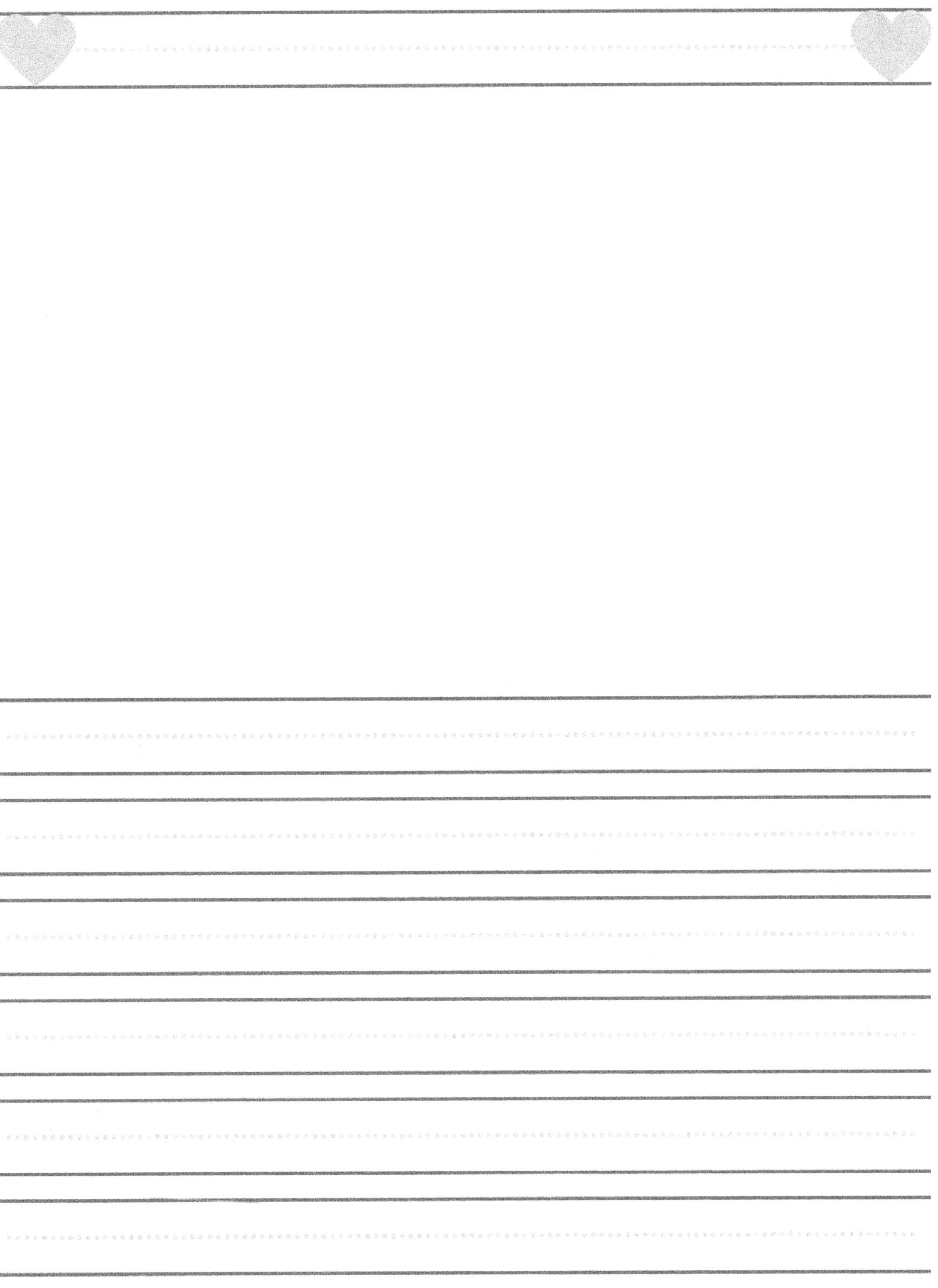

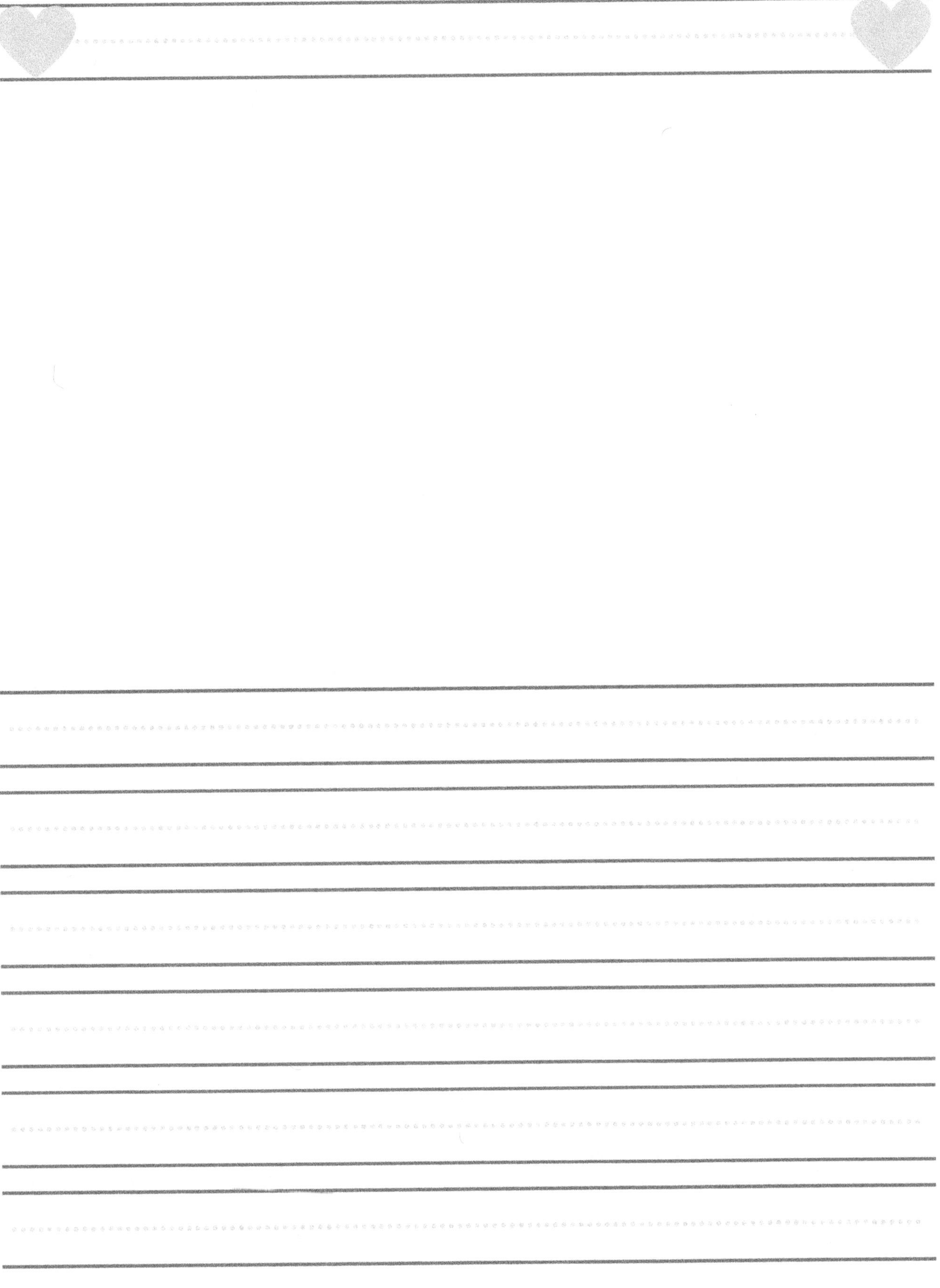

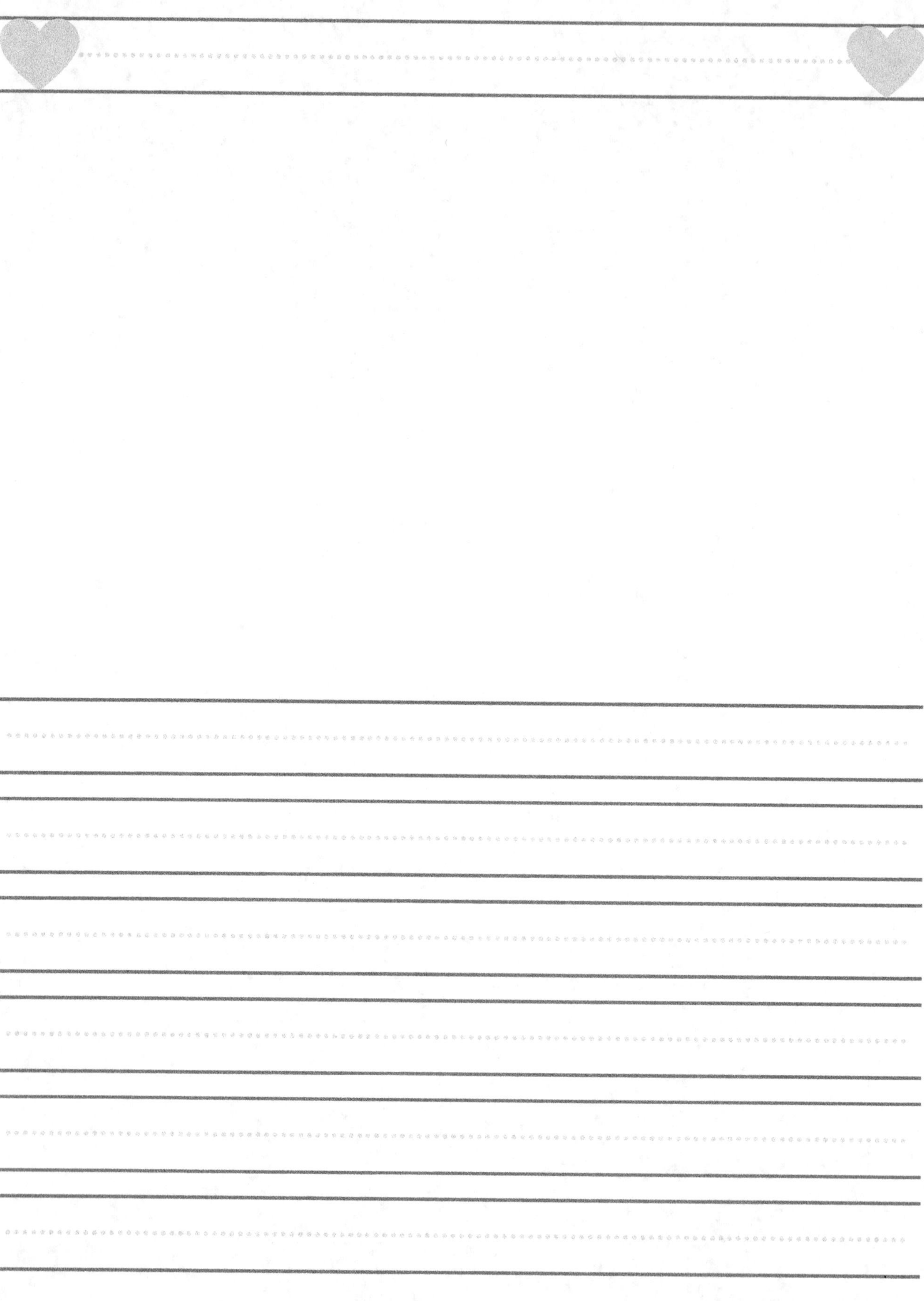

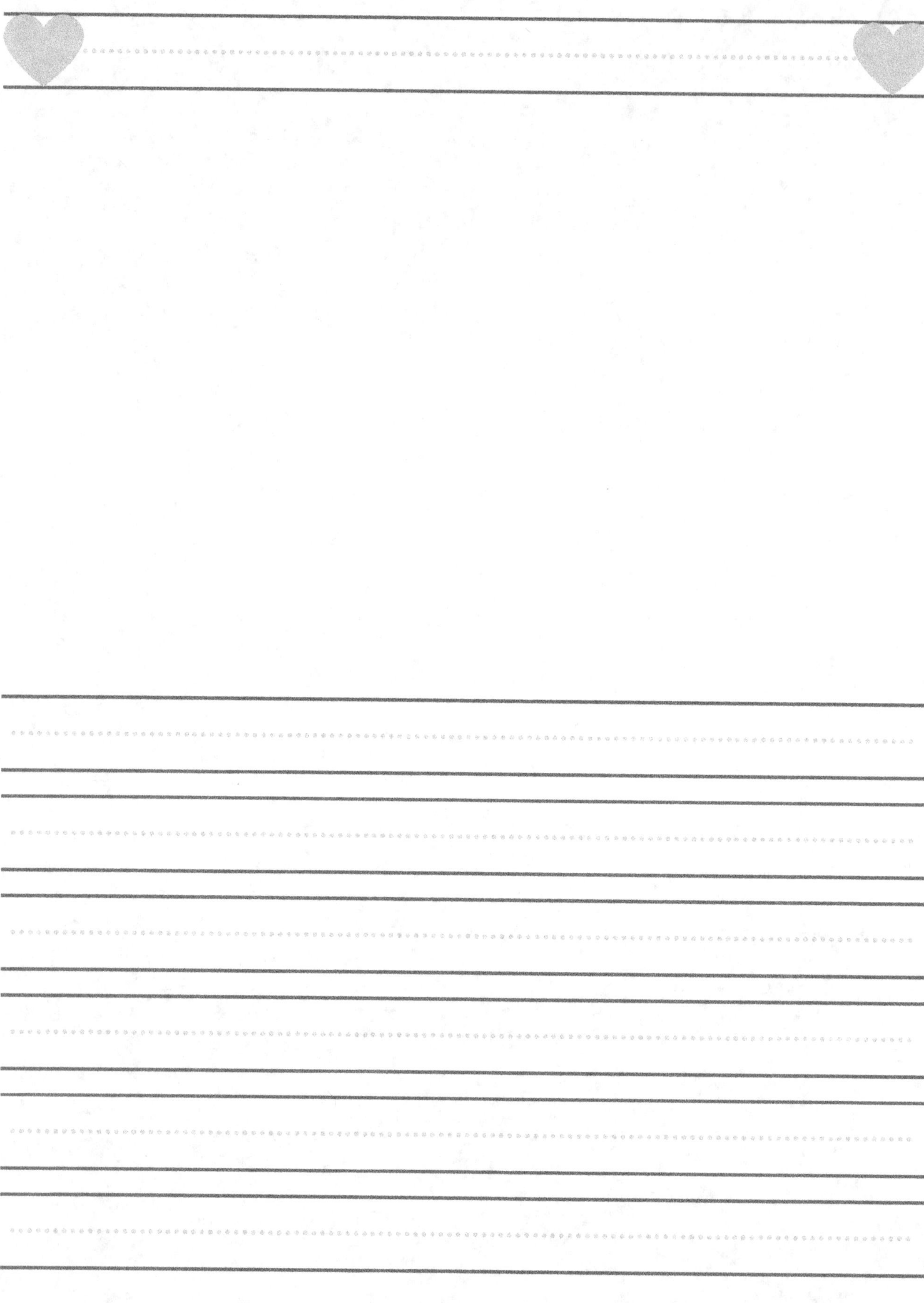

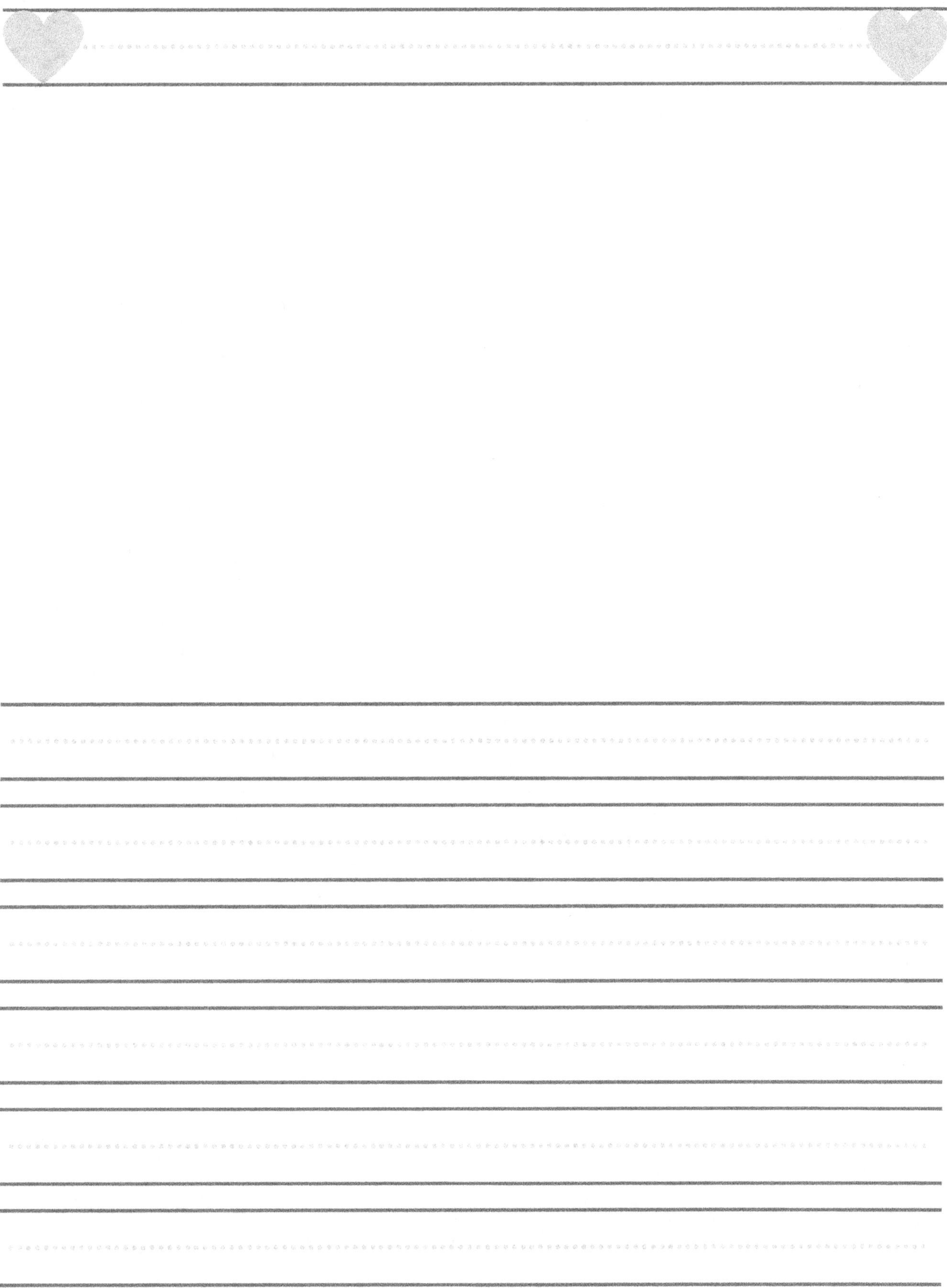

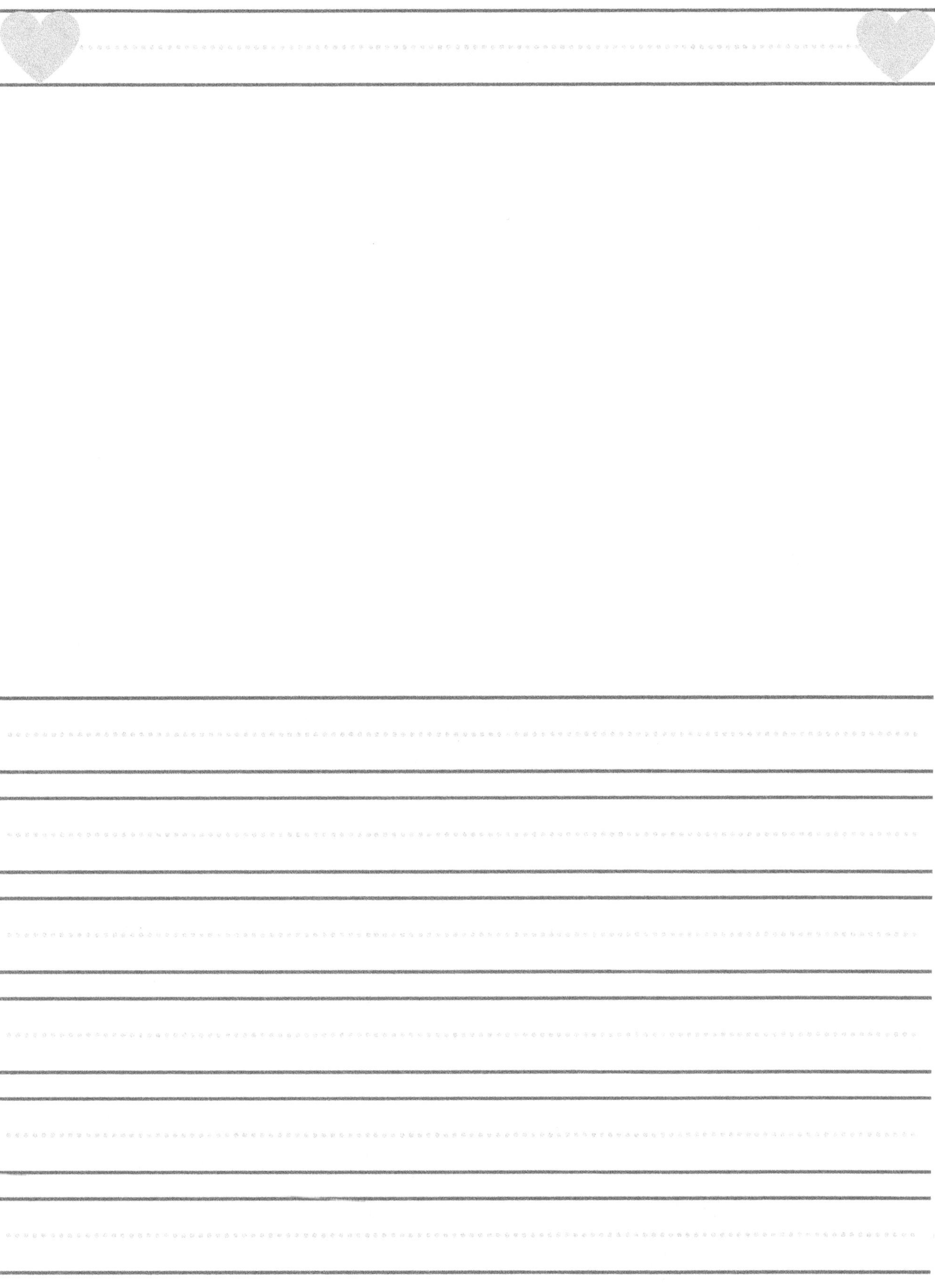

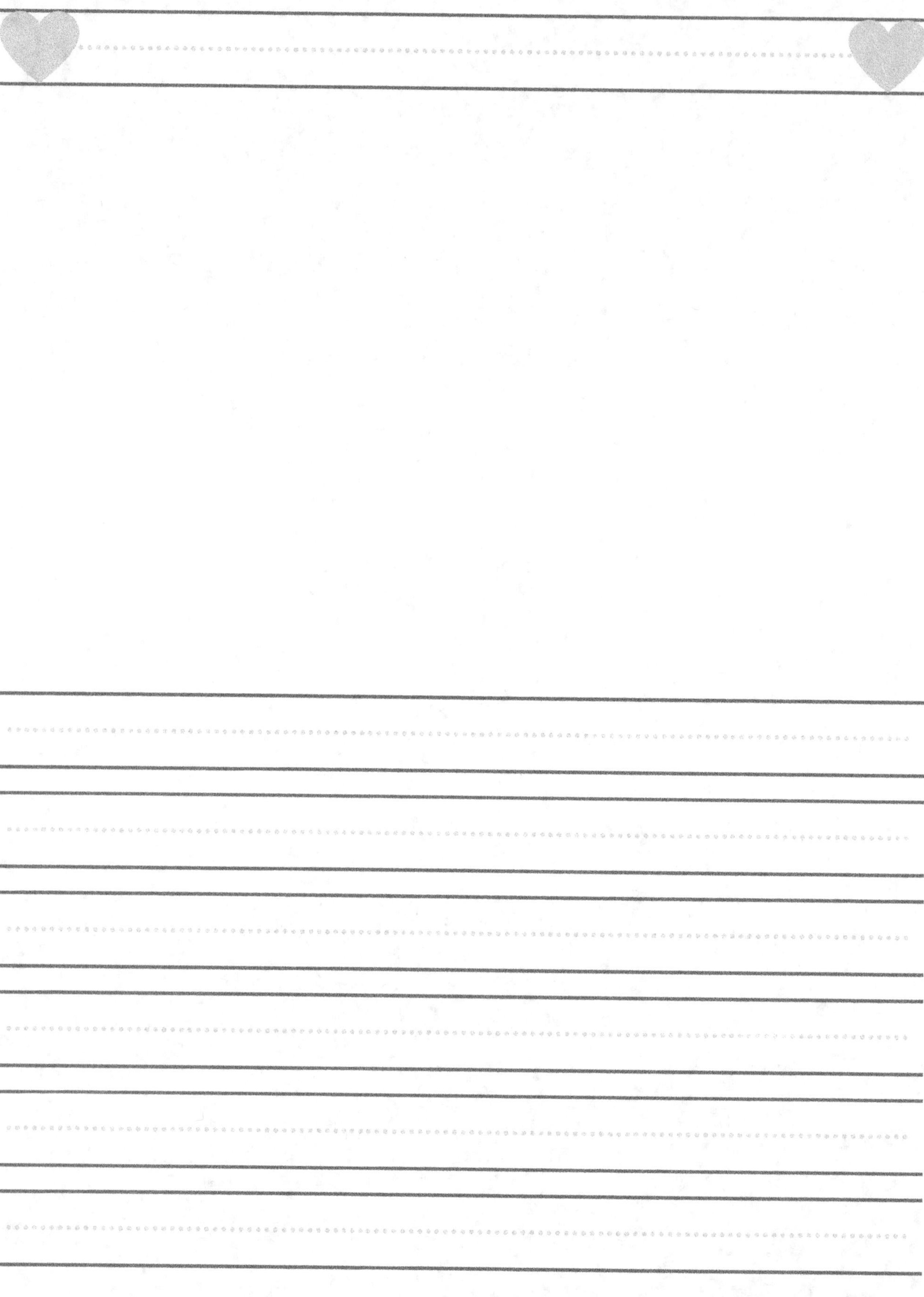

Email us at

agenzero9@gmail.com

to get free extras

---

just title the email
"Dotted Midline"

and we will send someone extra
surprise your way!

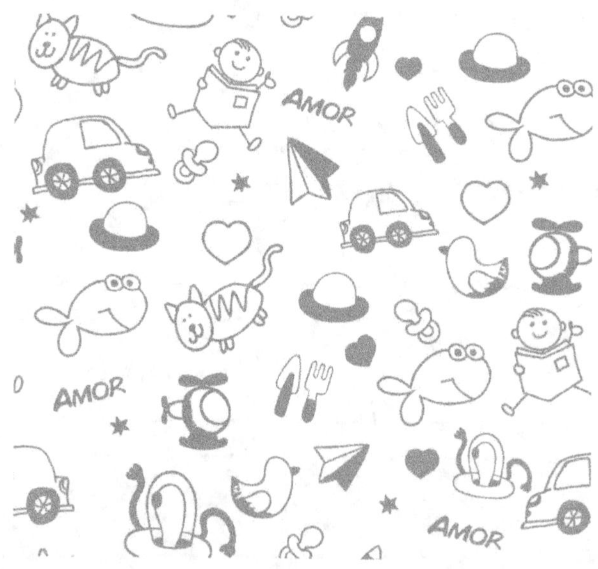